PEPPERIDGE FARM®

Easy Entertaining

Recipes for Family and Friends

Pepperidge Farm Easy Entertaining was produced by the Publishing Division of Campbell Soup Company, Campbell Place, Camden, NJ 08103-1799.

Senior Managing Editor:	Pat Teberg
Assistant Editors:	Ginny Gance, Peg Romano
Marketing Managers:	Joe Brennan, Margie Connors, Thomas Daly, Parker Gilbert, Melanie Thornberry, Greg Trepp
Public Relations Managers:	Ann Davin, Liz Gabriele, Elizabeth Hanlin, Leslie Weaver
Consumer Food Center:	Jackie Finch, Patricia Ward
Photography:	Peter Walters Photography/Chicago
Photographers:	Peter Walters, Peter Ross
Photo Stylist/Production:	Betty Karslake
Food Stylists:	Amy Andrews, Lois Hlavac, Moisette McNerney, Gail O'Donnell

Designed and published by Meredith Custom Publishing, 1912 Grand Avenue, Des Moines, IA 50309-3379. Printed in Hong Kong.

Pictured on the front cover (from left to right): Easy Lemon Chicken (*page 30*) and Strawberries Bonaparte (*page 84*).

Pictured on the back cover: Sesame Beef and Peppers (*page 48*).

Preparation and Cooking Times: Every recipe was developed and tested in the Campbell's Consumer Food Center by professional home economists. Use "Bake Time," "Chill Time," "Cook Time," "Prep Time" and/or "Thaw Time" given with each recipe as guides. The preparation times are based on the approximate amount of time required to assemble the recipe *before* baking or cooking. These times include preparation steps, such as chopping; mixing; cooking rice, pasta, vegetables; etc. The fact that some preparation steps can be done simultaneously or during cooking is taken into account. The cook times are based on the minimum amount of time required to cook, bake or broil the food in the recipes.

For sending us glassware, flatware, dinnerware, oven-to-tableware, cookware and serving accessories used in recipe photographs, a special thanks to: *Bernardaud New York, Inc.*, New York, NY on the front cover and pages 47, 63 and 83; *Christofle*, New York, NY on pages 47 and 81; *Dansk International Designs Ltd.*, Mount Kisco, NY on page 93; *Fitz and Floyd*, Dallas, TX on page 27; *Lenox China and Crystal*, Lawrenceville, NJ on page 43; *Mikasa*, Secaucus, NJ on page 85; *Mottahedeh*, New York, NY on page 7; *Nikko Ceramics, Inc.*, Wayne, NJ on pages 45 and 68-69; *Oneida Silversmiths*, Oneida, NY on pages 72-73, 75 and 93; *The Pfaltzgraff Co.*, York, PA on pages 55, 67 and 89; *Pickard Incorporated*, Antioch, IL on pages 76-77; *Reed & Barton Silversmiths*, Taunton, MA on pages 10-11 and 45; *Royal Worcester and Spode*, Moorestown, NJ on pages 9, 21, 41, 75 and 89; *Swid Powell*, New York, NY on page 35; *Taitù*, Dallas, TX on page 39; *Villeroy & Boch*, Princeton, NJ on page 87; *Wedgwood*, Wall, NJ on pages 53, 55, 57, 61 and 65; and *Yamazaki Tableware*, Teterboro, NJ on pages 41, 65, 83 and 85.

Easy Entertaining

The Spirit of '37

A Commitment to Quality Passed on Through the Years

Lemon Tarts (top, recipe page 90) and Ham-and-Cheese Florentine (bottom, recipe page 60)

*H*ere on these pages, you'll find old Pepperidge Farm favorites and innovatively delicious new ideas that have been developed into memorable recipes for easy family meals and entertaining. When you share the homemade taste and old-fashioned goodness of Pepperidge Farm recipes with special people, you'll experience the commitment to quality upon which Pepperidge Farm was born...in the small kitchen of a very determined woman.

Margaret Rudkin of Fairfield, Connecticut, was a woman with a mission. When she couldn't find a wholesome, all-natural loaf of commercial bread on the market to serve her family, the 40-year-old housewife and mother of three boys took matters into her own hands and created her own whole wheat bread with only the purest and finest of ingredients. It is that original, naturally delicious loaf of bread, combined with a mother's devoted determination, that has come to symbolize the heartfelt heritage of goodness known as Pepperidge Farm.

Named for the stately Pepperidge trees that framed her home in the Fairfield countryside, Pepperidge Farm was born in 1937 when Mrs. Rudkin's modest enterprise outgrew her kitchen — as well as the consumer demand for her whole wheat bread with the home-baked quality. Mrs. Rudkin expanded her uncompromising commitment to wholesome bakery freshness when she later introduced premium stuffings, puff pastry, cookies and crackers.

In 1961, Pepperidge Farm joined the Campbell Soup family. Margaret Rudkin devotedly continued to serve as Pepperidge Farm's chairman until she retired in 1966. Her determined spirit and

Above: Margaret Rudkin. Left: Pepperidge Farm Old Mill. Far Left: Pepperidge Farm's "Country Gentleman," actor Charlie Welch, has been charming television viewers since 1977.

dedication to quality remain key ingredients in the Pepperidge Farm products you buy today.

5

Say it Simply with Pepperidge Farm...

It's the holiday season. It's graduation time. It's a special birthday. These are the times when family and friends gather together to celebrate and enjoy good food. When it comes to serving the best food to your guests, you can rely on this cookbook from Pepperidge Farm for dozens of easy-to-prepare, great-tasting recipes. For those times when unexpected guests stop by, plan ahead by keeping a box of Pepperidge Farm crackers and Pepperidge Farm cookies on the pantry shelf. Here are some delicious and fast-to-fix ideas for *easy entertaining* with Pepperidge Farm crackers and cookies.

Simple Beginnings — Crackers and Cheese

Pepperidge Farm Distinctive Three Cracker Assortment offers a variety of crackers, so everyone can enjoy their favorites—Hearty Wheat Crackers, English Water Crackers and Butter Thins Crackers. Here are a few cheeses to consider serving with these delicious crackers.

• **Blue** has a piquant flavor with an edible blue-green mold marbled throughout its white interior. Good with crackers and fruit and in salads.

• **Boursin** is a French triple crème cheese with a pure white color. Often sold flavored. Good with breads and crackers.

• **Brie** is soft with a buttery interior and white edible rind. Good with crackers and in cooking.

• **Camembert** is milder in flavor than Brie. Good with crackers and fruit.

• **Cheddar** has a mild flavor when young; sharpness increases as it ages. Good with fruit and crackers and in cooking.

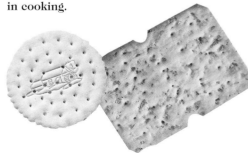

• **Gouda** and **Edam** have smooth textures with mild, nutty flavors. Gouda is made from whole milk. Edam is made from part-skim milk. Both are good for snacking with crackers.

• **Fontina** has a creamy, silky texture with a mild buttery flavor. Good with crackers and in cooking.

• **Havarti** is a creamy semisoft cheese with a mild flavor when young. This cheese is good with fruit and crackers and for melting.

• **Swiss** is mild in flavor with large holes. Good with crackers and in cooking.

Quick Cracker Bites

Top your favorite Pepperidge Farm cracker with your choice of:

- Cheese slices garnished with apple wedges

- Kiwi fruit and strawberry slices

- Cottage cheese sprinkled with chopped fruit or vegetables

- Slices of hard-cooked eggs

- Cream cheese topped with chutney

- Pear slices topped with Brie, then run under the broiler

- Apple butter sprinkled with snipped dried fruit

- Prepared cheese spread or pâté

Simple Endings — Cookies and Coffee

When unexpected family or friends stop by to visit, the sweet, simple solution is to serve them Pepperidge Farm cookies and steaming cups of coffee or tall glasses of cold milk.

Let the experienced bakers make the cookies, especially for spur-of-the-moment holiday entertaining. European heritage and American ingenuity combine to make *Pepperidge Farm* Distinctive cookies. Nowhere else will you find as elaborate a selection of delicious cookie varieties as with Pepperidge Farm. Our most popular Distinctive cookies are *Milano*, *Bordeaux*, Chessmen, *Brussels* and *Geneva*.

For casual occasions, open a bag of *Pepperidge Farm American Collection* cookies. Pepperidge Farm bakers make these cookies big and lumpy bumpy. Only the best of the best ingredients are used to make *Sausalito*, Nantucket and Chesapeake. If you prefer soft cookies, you can find the same quality ingredients in our Soft Baked cookie varieties like Chocolate Chunk, Milk Chocolate Macadamia and Oatmeal Raisin cookies.

Serve only the best to your family and friends— serve them Pepperidge Farm cookies.

Incredible Pastry. Incredibly Easy.

In keeping with tradition—top-quality products and fine baking heritage—the European pastry chefs at Pepperidge Farm perfected a recipe for ready-made puff pastry dough. This pastry "puffs" as it bakes into dozens of flaky, golden layers yielding a light, tender and delicate pastry.

Pepperidge Farm manufactures their top-quality pastry in two easy-to-use forms: puff pastry shells and puff pastry sheets. The pastry shells are precut into six individual shells. The pastry sheets are prerolled and are ready to use. Both can be found in the freezer section at the grocery store.

Unlike puff pastry made from scratch, this puff pastry is not difficult to use. Read on and see for yourself how incredibly easy it is to use Pepperidge Farm puff pastry.

Puff Pastry Shells

The pastry shells are precut into six individual servings. They are ready to bake right from the package.

• Remove as many pastry shells as needed. Rewrap unused pastry shells in plastic wrap or foil and return to freezer. Place pastry shells on ungreased baking sheet with the word "top" facing up. Place shells about two inches apart on baking sheet.

• Always bake pastry shells in a preheated 400°F. oven. Do not bake shells in a microwave or a toaster oven. If the shells are cooking unevenly, turn the baking sheet or move the baking sheet to a different rack for more even browning.

• Bake shells about 20 to 25 minutes until golden brown. Then remove "top" and soft pastry underneath. Return shells to oven 3 to 5 minutes for extra crispness. The top may be used as garnish. (Unfilled baked shells may be stored in an airtight container at room temperature for up to two days. Recrisp shells in a 400°F. oven for 5 minutes.)

Puff Pastry Sheets

The prerolled pastry sheets are folded into thirds and come two to a package. The sheets must be thawed before using.

Thawing pastry sheets
• Remove as many pastry sheets as needed. Rewrap unused pastry in plastic wrap or foil and return to freezer.

• Quick Thaw—Separate pastry sheets. Cover each pastry sheet with a piece of plastic wrap and thaw at room temperature about 30 minutes before unfolding.

• Refrigerator Thaw—Wrap pastry sheet in plastic wrap. Thaw 1 pastry sheet in the refrigerator about 4 hours. A whole package thaws in about 6 hours.

• Thawed pastry should be cool to the touch and will unfold without breaking.

• Thawed pastry sheets can be refrigerated up to two days.

Shaping pastry sheets

• Work with 1 pastry sheet at a time, keeping the other in the refrigerator.

• Roll pastry sheet on a lightly floured board, countertop or pastry cloth.

• Handle pastry as little as possible to ensure tenderness.

• Use a ruler to measure rolled pastry.

• If pastry gets too soft, return it to the refrigerator to chill for a few minutes.

• Cut pastry with a sharp cutting utensil such as a sharp knife or a pastry or pizza wheel.

• Seal edges of filled pastries or turnovers together by pressing edges with a fork or sealing edges with pastry crimper and sealer.

Baking pastry sheets

• Bake pastry sheets in a preheated oven.

• Dark glazed baking sheets may bake puff pastry faster; adjust bake time if necessary.

• About halfway through baking, peek into the oven to see how the pastry is baking. If the pastry is cooking unevenly, turn the baking sheet or move the baking sheet to a different rack for more even browning.

Sausage Rolls
(page 25)

Easy Fix-ups

Thaw pastry sheet(s) as package directs. Preheat oven to 400°F. Unfold pastry and proceed with a serving suggestion below. Bake pastry for 10 minutes or until golden.

• **Pastry Cut-Outs:** Cut pastry into squares or circles and bake. *For main dishes,* top with saucy entrées. *For desserts,* top with cut-up fresh fruit, pie filling or scoops of ice cream.

• **Sweet Treats:** Brush pastry with 1 egg beaten with 1 tablespoon water. Sprinkle with cinnamon-sugar mixture. Cut pastry into strips, bake and serve.

• **Savory Bites:** Brush pastry with 1 egg beaten with 1 tablespoon water. Sprinkle with herbs, cheese *and/or* spices. Cut pastry into small shapes, bake and serve. Use as snacks, croutons or float in your favorite soup or chowder.

Festive Finger Foods

Once the guests have arrived, it's up to you to set the stage for their party time enjoyment! With a minimum of preparation and Pepperidge Farm frozen Puff Pastry, recipes such as *Ham-and-Broccoli Swirls* and *Parmesan Crisps*, to name a few, will create a swirl of excitement all their own. And, *Franks Under Wraps* won't be around for long when your friends and family discover this fun, flavorful finger food!

Pictured clockwise from top right: *Nacho Cheese Bites* (page 12), *Parmesan Crisps* (page 14), *Spreadable Deviled Eggs* (page 16) and *Ham-and-Broccoli Swirls* (page 13).

Nacho Cheese Bites

½ package PEPPERIDGE FARM frozen Puff Pastry Sheets (1 sheet)
1 egg, beaten
1 tablespoon water
1 cup shredded Cheddar cheese (4 ounces)
¼ cup PACE Thick & Chunky Salsa
5 VLASIC or EARLY CALIFORNIA pitted Ripe Olives, cut into quarters (optional)
   Chili powder

• Thaw pastry sheet at room temperature 30 minutes. Preheat oven to 400°F. Mix egg and water and set aside. Mix cheese and salsa and set aside.

• Unfold pastry on lightly floured surface. Roll into 15- by 12-inch rectangle. Cut into 20 (3-inch) squares. Place about *1 tablespoon* cheese mixture in center of each square. Top with olive piece (*fig. A*). Brush edges of squares with egg mixture. Fold squares to form triangles (*fig. B*). Seal edges with fork (*fig. C*). Place 2 inches apart on baking sheet. Brush with egg mixture and sprinkle with chili powder.

• Bake 15 minutes or until golden. Serve warm or at room temperature.

Makes 20 appetizers • Thaw Time: 30 minutes
Prep Time: 15 minutes • Cook Time: 15 minutes

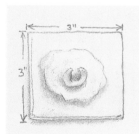

A. Top cheese mixture with olive piece.

B. Fold squares to form triangles.

C. Seal edges with fork.

Ham-and-Broccoli Swirls

½ package PEPPERIDGE FARM frozen Puff Pastry Sheets (1 sheet)
1 egg, beaten
1 tablespoon water
1 container (4 ounces) whipped cream cheese with chives spread
1 package (10 ounces) frozen chopped broccoli (2 cups), thawed
and well drained
1 cup finely chopped cooked ham

• Thaw pastry sheet at room temperature 30 minutes. Preheat oven to 400°F. Mix egg and water and set aside.

• Unfold pastry on lightly floured surface. Roll into 16- by 12-inch rectangle. Spread cream cheese over rectangle to within ½ inch of edges. Top with broccoli and ham *(fig. A)*. Starting at long side, roll up like a jelly roll, only to center. Roll up opposite side to center *(fig. B)*. Brush between rolls with egg mixture, then gently press rolls together. Cut into 32 (½-inch) slices *(fig. C)*. Place 2 inches apart on greased baking sheet. Brush tops with egg mixture.

• Bake 15 minutes or until golden. Serve warm or at room temperature.

Makes 32 appetizers • Thaw Time: 30 minutes
Prep Time: 20 minutes • Cook Time: 15 minutes

TIP: To make ahead, cut into slices and place on baking sheet. Freeze. When frozen, store in plastic bag up to one month. To bake, place frozen slices on baking sheet and bake at 400°F. for 20 minutes or until golden.

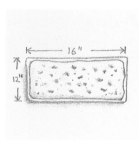

A. Top cream cheese with broccoli and ham.

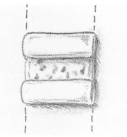

B. Roll up both sides to center, like a jelly roll.

C. Cut into ½-inch slices.

Parmesan Crisps

½ package PEPPERIDGE FARM frozen Puff Pastry Sheets (1 sheet)
1 egg, beaten
1 tablespoon water
¼ cup grated Parmesan cheese
1 tablespoon chopped fresh parsley or 1 teaspoon dried parsley flakes
½ teaspoon dried oregano leaves, crushed

• Thaw pastry sheet at room temperature 30 minutes. Preheat oven to 400°F. Mix egg and water and set aside. Mix cheese, parsley and oregano and set aside.

• Unfold pastry on lightly floured surface. Roll into 14- by 10-inch rectangle. Cut in half lengthwise. Brush both halves with egg mixture. Top 1 rectangle with cheese mixture. Place remaining rectangle over cheese-topped rectangle, egg-side down. Roll gently with rolling pin to seal (fig. A).

• Cut crosswise into 28 (½-inch) strips (fig. B). Twist strips and place 2 inches apart on greased baking sheet, pressing down ends (fig. C). Brush with egg mixture.

• Bake 10 minutes or until golden. Serve warm or at room temperature.

Makes 28 appetizers • Thaw Time: 30 minutes
Prep Time: 20 minutes • Cook Time: 10 minutes

TIP: Parmesan Crisps can be stored in airtight container up to one week.

A. Roll gently with rolling pin to seal.

B. Cut crosswise into 28 (½-inch) strips.

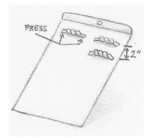

C. Twist strips and place 2 inches apart on greased baking sheet, pressing down ends.

Franks Under Wraps

½ package PEPPERIDGE FARM frozen Puff Pastry Sheets (1 sheet)
1 egg, beaten
1 tablespoon water
10 frankfurters (about 1 pound), cut crosswise into halves
    Prepared mustard

• Thaw pastry sheet at room temperature 30 minutes. Preheat oven to 400°F. Mix egg and water and set aside.

• Unfold pastry on lightly floured surface. Cut into 20 (½-inch) strips. Wrap pastry strips around frankfurters, pressing gently to seal *(fig. A)*. Place 2 inches apart on baking sheet. Brush with egg mixture *(fig. B)*.

• Bake 15 minutes or until golden. Serve with mustard for dipping.

Makes 20 appetizers • Thaw Time: 30 minutes
Prep Time: 15 minutes • Cook Time: 15 minutes

A. Wrap pastry strips around frankfurters, pressing gently to seal.

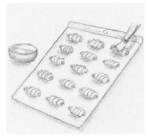

B. Brush each with some egg mixture.

Spinach-Almond Dip

    1 pouch CAMPBELL'S Dry Onion with Chicken Broth Soup and Recipe Mix
    1 container (16 ounces) sour cream
    1 package (about 10 ounces) frozen chopped spinach, thawed and well drained
    ⅓ cup chopped toasted almonds
       PEPPERIDGE FARM Distinctive Three Cracker Assortment
         and/or Sesame Crackers

• Mix soup mix, sour cream, spinach and almonds. Cover and refrigerate at least 2 hours.

• Serve with crackers for dipping. If desired, garnish with *tomatoes* and *fresh basil*.

Makes about 2½ cups • Prep Time: 10 minutes
Chill Time: 2 hours

Spreadable Deviled Eggs

    4 hard-cooked eggs
    ¼ cup mayonnaise
    1 tablespoon Dijon-style mustard
    1 teaspoon finely chopped onion
    1 teaspoon chopped fresh parsley or ¼ teaspoon dried parsley flakes
       PEPPERIDGE FARM Distinctive Butter Thins and/or Hearty Wheat Crackers

• Cut eggs in half. Remove yolks. Mash yolks and *1 egg white* with fork. Stir in mayonnaise, mustard, onion and *1 teaspoon* parsley. Coarsely chop remaining 3 egg whites.

• Place chopped egg whites in a 5-inch circle on serving plate. Spread egg yolk mixture on top. Cover and refrigerate at least 2 hours. Serve with crackers. If desired, garnish with *radishes* and *fresh parsley*.

Makes about 1¼ cups • Prep Time: 35 minutes
Chill Time: 2 hours

Salmon-Dill Dip

    1 package (8 ounces) cream cheese, softened
    1 can (about 6 to 8 ounces) salmon, drained
    1 tablespoon lemon juice
    ½ teaspoon dried dill weed, crushed
    ¼ teaspoon prepared horseradish
        PEPPERIDGE FARM Distinctive Three Cracker Assortment
        and/or Sesame Crackers

• Mix cream cheese, salmon, lemon juice, dill and horseradish. Cover and refrigerate at least
2 hours. Serve with crackers for dipping. If desired, garnish with *fresh chives* and *fresh tarragon.*

Makes about 1⅓ cups • Prep Time: 10 minutes
Chill Time: 2 hours

Two-Pepper Pizza

    ½ package PEPPERIDGE FARM frozen Puff Pastry Sheets (1 sheet)
        Garlic powder
    1 cup shredded mozzarella cheese (4 ounces)
    ¼ cup sliced VLASIC or EARLY CALIFORNIA pitted Ripe Olives
    ¼ cup finely chopped green and sweet red pepper
    ¼ teaspoon dried oregano leaves, crushed

• Thaw pastry sheet at room temperature 30 minutes. Preheat oven to 400°F.

• Unfold pastry on lightly floured surface. Roll into 15- by 10-inch rectangle. Cut in half
lengthwise and place on baking sheet. Prick with fork. Sprinkle with garlic powder.
Bake 10 minutes.

• Top with cheese, olives, pepper and oregano. Bake 5 minutes more or until cheese is melted.
Cut each pizza into 16 squares. If desired, garnish with *fresh oregano.*

Makes 32 appetizers • Thaw Time: 30 minutes
Prep Time: 20 minutes • Cook Time: 15 minutes

Salmon-Dill Dip *(top)*
Two-Pepper Pizza *(bottom)*

Garden Vegetable Spread

1 package (8 ounces) cream cheese, softened
½ cup chopped cucumber
1 medium carrot, shredded (about ½ cup)
1 green onion, chopped (about 2 tablespoons)
1 teaspoon lemon juice
¼ teaspoon dried dill weed, crushed or 1 teaspoon chopped fresh dill weed
   PEPPERIDGE FARM Distinctive Three Cracker Assortment
    and/or Sesame Crackers

• Mix cream cheese, cucumber, carrot, onion, lemon juice and dill. Cover and refrigerate at least 2 hours. Serve with crackers. If desired, garnish with *cucumber, carrot* and *fresh dill.*

Makes about 1½ cups • Prep Time: 10 minutes
Chill Time: 2 hours

Crab Melt

1 package (8 ounces) cream cheese, softened
1 can (about 6 ounces) white crab meat, drained
¼ cup mayonnaise
1 tablespoon finely chopped onion
1 teaspoon prepared mustard
1 teaspoon Worcestershire sauce
   Paprika
   PEPPERIDGE FARM Distinctive Hearty Wheat and/or Butter Thins Crackers

• In 9-inch pie plate or 2-cup oven-safe casserole, mix cream cheese, crab, mayonnaise, onion, mustard and Worcestershire sauce. Sprinkle with paprika.

• Bake at 350°F. for 15 minutes or until hot. Serve with crackers. If desired, garnish with *lemon, fresh chives* and *edible flowers.*

Makes about 2 cups • Prep Time: 10 minutes
Cook Time: 15 minutes

TIP: In 2-cup microwave-safe casserole, mix cream cheese, crab, mayonnaise, onion, mustard and Worcestershire. Microwave on HIGH 2 minutes. Stir. Microwave 2 minutes more. Sprinkle with paprika. Serve with crackers.

Garden Vegetable Spread (*top*)
Crab Melt (*bottom*)

Lemon-Pepper Cheese Wheel

1 package (10 ¼ ounces) **PEPPERIDGE FARM** *Distinctive Hearty Wheat Crackers*
3 packages (8 ounces each) cream cheese, softened
4 eggs
½ cup milk
1 cup shredded Swiss cheese (4 ounces)
¼ cup grated Parmesan cheese
2 green onions, chopped (about ¼ cup)
1 teaspoon freshly ground pepper
1 teaspoon grated lemon peel

• Preheat oven to 350°F. Crush 20 crackers in plastic bag with rolling pin. Spread evenly in bottom of 9-inch springform pan and set aside.

• In food processor or large bowl place cream cheese, eggs and milk. Cover and blend in food processor or beat with electric mixer at medium speed until smooth. Add Swiss cheese, Parmesan cheese, onions, pepper and lemon peel. Blend or beat to mix well. Pour into prepared springform pan.

• Bake 1 hour or until golden. Cool in pan on wire rack. Cover and refrigerate at least 4 hours or overnight. Serve with remaining crackers. If desired, garnish with *lemon* and *fresh mint*.

Makes 16 appetizer servings • Prep Time: 20 minutes
Cook Time: 1 hour • Chill Time: 4 hours

Savory Stuffed Mushrooms

    24 medium fresh mushrooms (about 1 pound)
     6 tablespoons margarine or butter
    ¼ cup chopped onion (about 1 small)
    ¼ teaspoon garlic powder or 2 cloves garlic, minced
     1 cup PEPPERIDGE FARM Herb Seasoned Stuffing
     1 package (3 ounces) cream cheese, softened
     3 tablespoons grated Parmesan cheese
     2 tablespoons chopped fresh parsley or 2 teaspoons dried parsley flakes

• Remove stems from mushrooms. Chop enough stems to make *1 cup* and set aside.

• In medium saucepan over medium heat, heat *2 tablespoons* margarine. Brush mushroom caps with margarine and place top-side down in shallow baking pan. Heat remaining margarine. Add chopped mushroom stems, onion and garlic powder and cook until tender.

• Add stuffing, cream cheese, Parmesan cheese and parsley. Mix lightly. Spoon about *1 tablespoon* stuffing mixture into each mushroom cap.

• Bake at 425°F. for 10 minutes or until mushrooms are heated through. If desired, garnish with *assorted sweet peppers.*

Makes 24 appetizers • Prep Time: 25 minutes
Cook Time: 10 minutes

TIP: Cut a thin slice from top of each mushroom cap so mushrooms are level.

TIP: After mushrooms are stuffed, cover and refrigerate for up to 24 hours. Bake as directed.

Walnut-Cheddar Ball

    2 cups shredded Cheddar cheese (8 ounces)
    ½ cup finely chopped walnuts
    ¼ cup mayonnaise
    1 green onion, chopped (about 2 tablespoons)
    1 tablespoon Dijon-style mustard
    1 teaspoon Worcestershire sauce
    ¼ cup chopped fresh parsley
        PEPPERIDGE FARM Distinctive Three Cracker Assortment
            and/or Sesame Crackers

• Mix cheese, walnuts, mayonnaise, onion, mustard and Worcestershire sauce. Shape mixture into ball. Roll in parsley to coat. Cover and refrigerate at least 2 hours. Serve with crackers. If desired, garnish with *fresh sage.*

Makes about 2 cups • Prep Time: 20 minutes
Chill Time: 2 hours

Sausage Rolls

    ½ package PEPPERIDGE FARM frozen Puff Pastry Sheets (1 sheet)
    ½ pound bulk pork sausage

• Thaw pastry sheet at room temperature 30 minutes. Preheat oven to 400°F.

• Unfold pastry on lightly floured surface. Roll into 12- by 10-inch rectangle. Cut into 3 (3-inch) strips.

• Divide sausage into thirds. Roll each third into a cylinder the length of the pastry. Place on edge of pastry strip. Starting at the long side, roll up. Press edges to seal.

• Cut each roll into 12 (1-inch) slices. Place 1½ inches apart on baking sheet. Bake 15 minutes or until golden. If desired, garnish with *carrot curl* and *fresh herbs.*

Makes 36 appetizers • Thaw Time: 30 minutes
Prep Time: 20 minutes • Cook Time: 15 minutes

Spinach-Cheese Swirls

½ package PEPPERIDGE FARM *frozen Puff Pastry Sheets (1 sheet)*
1 egg, beaten
1 tablespoon water
½ cup shredded Muenster or Monterey Jack cheese (2 ounces)
¼ cup grated Parmesan cheese
1 green onion, chopped (about 2 tablespoons)
⅛ teaspoon garlic powder
1 package (about 10 ounces) frozen chopped spinach, thawed and well drained

• Thaw pastry at room temperature 30 minutes. Preheat oven to 400°F. Mix egg and water and set aside. Mix Muenster cheese, Parmesan cheese, onion and garlic powder and set aside.

• Unfold pastry on lightly floured surface. Brush with egg mixture. Top with cheese mixture and spinach. Starting at one side, roll up like a jelly roll *(fig. A)*. Cut into 20 (½-inch) slices. Place 2 inches apart on baking sheet *(fig. B)*. Brush tops with egg mixture.

• Bake 15 minutes or until golden.

Makes 20 appetizers • Thaw Time: 30 minutes
Prep Time: 20 minutes • Cook Time: 15 minutes

A. Starting at one side, roll up like a jelly roll.

B. Place 2 inches apart on baking sheet.

Walnut-Cheddar Ball *(top, recipe page 25)*
Spinach-Cheese Swirls *(center)*
Savory Stuffed Mushrooms *(bottom, recipe page 24)*

Amazing Main Dishes

Entertaining with old-fashioned flavor and flair is a no-fuss affair! When you serve timelessly delicious and easy recipes like *Cheddary Chicken and Broccoli, Chicken Pot Pie* and *Sweet-and-Sour Stuffed Pork Chops,* family and guests get the V.I.P. treatment—you get the glory!

Pastry Tostadas Olé (left, page 56) and *Golden Chicken and Vegetables* (right, page 31).

Easy Lemon Chicken

1 package **PEPPERIDGE FARM** frozen *Puff Pastry Shells*
1 tablespoon *vegetable oil*
1 pound *skinless, boneless chicken breasts, cut into cubes*
2 jars (12 ounces each) **PEPPERIDGE FARM** *Golden Chicken Gravy*
2 tablespoons *lemon juice*
¼ teaspoon *dried thyme leaves, crushed*
3 cups *cooked cut-up vegetables or 1 bag (16 ounces) frozen vegetable combination, cooked and drained*

• Bake pastry shells according to package directions.

• In medium skillet over medium-high heat, heat oil. Add chicken in 2 batches and cook until browned, stirring often. Set chicken aside. Pour off fat.

• Add gravy, lemon juice, thyme and vegetables. Heat to a boil. Return chicken to pan. Reduce heat to low. Cover and cook 5 minutes or until chicken is no longer pink.

• Serve in pastry shells. If desired, garnish with *fresh thyme*.

Makes 6 servings • Bake Time: 30 minutes
Prep Time: 20 minutes • Cook Time: 20 minutes

Golden Chicken and Vegetables

   2 tablespoons margarine or butter
   4 skinless, boneless chicken breast halves (about 1 pound)
   4 to 5 medium new potatoes (about 1 pound), sliced 1/4-inch thick
   1 medium onion, sliced (about 3/4 cup)
 1/4 teaspoon garlic powder or 2 cloves garlic, minced
   1 teaspoon dried thyme leaves, crushed
   1 jar (12 ounces) PEPPERIDGE FARM Golden Chicken Gravy
   2 tablespoons lemon juice
   1 cup frozen peas
 1/2 cup sour cream

• In medium skillet over medium-high heat, heat *half* the margarine. Add chicken and cook 10 minutes or until browned. Set chicken aside.

• Reduce heat to medium. Add remaining margarine. Add potatoes, onion, garlic powder and thyme. Cook 5 minutes or until browned, stirring occasionally.

• Add gravy and lemon juice. Heat to a boil. Cover and cook 20 minutes or until potatoes are tender.

• Return chicken to pan. Add peas. Reduce heat to low. Cover and cook 5 minutes or until chicken is no longer pink. Remove chicken to platter. Stir in sour cream. Serve potato mixture with chicken. If desired, garnish with *fresh parsley*.

Makes 4 servings • Prep Time: 15 minutes
Cook Time: 40 minutes

Turkey with all the Trimmings

When it's time for family and friends to gather 'round the table, rely on top-quality *Pepperidge Farm* stuffing and gravy to accompany your turkey. It takes great bread to make great stuffing. Pepperidge Farm bakes the finest blend of herbs and seasonings into their special stuffing breads. The best stocks brimming with meaty flavor and tender pieces of meat are used to make *Pepperidge Farm* gravy taste like homemade.

Here's how to make your next turkey dinner with all the trimmings a savory success! Start with a bag of Pepperidge Farm cubed country style stuffing, a jar of Pepperidge Farm seasoned turkey gravy and follow these directions.

Stuffing Tips

• Allow about ½ cup stuffing per pound of turkey or just enough stuffing to fill the turkey.
• Pack stuffing lightly in the turkey to allow room for expansion. As stuffing bakes, it absorbs juices and expands.
• Stuff the turkey just before roasting, *never ahead of time.*
• Extra stuffing may be baked separately in a covered casserole for last 30 minutes of roasting time. (For a crisp top, uncover for last 5 minutes.)
• After the turkey is done, check the stuffing temperature with a meat thermometer.

Fully cooked stuffing should reach 165°F.
• Remove stuffing from turkey *immediately* after dinner.
• Refrigerate leftover stuffing and use within two days. Or, freeze stuffing and use within two months.
• The U.S. Department of Agriculture operates a toll-free Meat & Poultry Hotline. The nationwide number is 1-800-535-4555. From 10 a.m. to 4 p.m., EST, Monday through Friday, home economists will answer meat and poultry questions. Callers in the Washington, DC, metropolitan area should dial 202-447-3333.

Pepperidge Farm Gravy— all the flavor of homemade without the work!

Pepperidge Farm gravy is made with natural meat stocks and juices and tender pieces of meat. Enjoy all seven 98% fat free varieties all year long!

Roast Turkey with Cranberry-Pecan Stuffing

¼ cup margarine or butter
2 ribs celery, sliced (about 1 cup)
1 large onion, chopped (about 1 cup)
1 can (14½ ounces) SWANSON Chicken Broth
1 bag (14 ounces) PEPPERIDGE FARM Cubed Country Style Stuffing
1 can (16 ounces) whole berry cranberry sauce
½ cup chopped pecans
12- to 14-pound turkey
    Vegetable oil
2 jars (12 ounces each) PEPPERIDGE FARM Seasoned Turkey Gravy

• In large saucepan over medium heat, heat margarine. Cook celery and onion until tender. Add broth. Heat to a boil. Remove from heat. Add stuffing, cranberry sauce and pecans. Mix lightly.

• Remove package of giblets and neck from turkey cavity. Rinse turkey with cold water and pat dry. Spoon stuffing lightly into neck and body cavities (*fig. A*). Fold loose skin over stuffing. (Bake any remaining stuffing in covered casserole dish along with turkey last 30 minutes of roasting or until hot.) Tie ends of drumsticks together. Place turkey, breast side up, on rack in shallow roasting pan. Brush with oil. Insert meat thermometer into thickest part of thigh, *not touching bone (fig. B)*.

• Roast at 325°F. for 4½ to 5 hours or until thermometer reads 180°F. and drumstick moves easily, basting occasionally with pan drippings. Begin checking doneness after 4 hours roasting time. When skin of turkey is golden brown, shield turkey loosely with foil to prevent overbrowning. Allow turkey to stand 10 minutes before slicing. Heat gravy and serve with turkey.

Makes about 9 cups stuffing or 12 to 16 servings
Prep Time: 30 minutes • Roast Time: 4½ to 5 hours

Lightly spoon stuffing into body cavity. *Do not pack.* As stuffing bakes it absorbs juices and expands.

Insert meat thermometer deep into thickest part of thigh next to body, *not touching bone.*

Pepper Parmesan Chicken

    4 chicken legs (about 2 pounds)
    1 jar (12 ounces) PEPPERIDGE FARM Golden Chicken
        or Cream of Chicken Gravy
    2 cups PEPPERIDGE FARM Home Style Cracked Pepper and Parmesan
        Cheese Croutons, crushed
    2 tablespoons margarine or butter, melted

• Dip chicken into ½ cup gravy. Coat with crouton crumbs.

• Place chicken in shallow baking pan. Drizzle with margarine. Bake at 375°F. for 1 hour or until chicken is no longer pink.

• Heat remaining gravy and serve with chicken.

Makes 4 servings • Prep Time: 10 minutes
Cook Time: 1 hour

Cheddary Chicken and Broccoli

    1 package PEPPERIDGE FARM frozen Puff Pastry Shells
    2 jars (12 ounces each) PEPPERIDGE FARM Golden Chicken Gravy
    1 tablespoon lemon juice
    2 cups frozen broccoli cuts, thawed
    2 cups cubed cooked chicken
    ½ cup shredded Cheddar cheese (2 ounces)
    ¼ cup PEPPERIDGE FARM Home Style Sourdough Cheese
        Croutons, crushed (optional)

• Bake pastry shells according to package directions.

• In large saucepan mix gravy, lemon juice, broccoli and chicken. Over medium heat, heat through, stirring occasionally.

• Serve in pastry shells. Sprinkle with cheese and top with crouton crumbs. If desired, garnish with *fresh chives* and *fresh rosemary*.

Makes 6 servings • Bake Time: 30 minutes
Prep Time: 15 minutes • Cook Time: 10 minutes

Pepper Parmesan Chicken *(top)*
Cheddary Chicken and Broccoli *(bottom)*

Nacho Chicken Potatoes

1 jar (12 ounces) **PEPPERIDGE FARM** Golden Chicken, Cream of Chicken or Seasoned Turkey Gravy
2 cups cubed cooked chicken or turkey
1 teaspoon chili powder
4 hot baked potatoes, split
1 medium tomato, chopped (about 1 cup)
½ cup shredded Cheddar cheese (2 ounces)
¼ cup sliced **VLASIC** or **EARLY CALIFORNIA** pitted Ripe Olives
1 green onion, sliced (about 2 tablespoons)

• In medium saucepan mix gravy, chicken and chili powder. Over medium heat, heat through.

• Serve over potatoes. Top with tomato, cheese, olives and onion. If desired, garnish with *radishes, green onions* and *fresh herbs.*

Makes 4 servings • Prep Time: 15 minutes
Cook Time: 5 minutes

TIP: Substitute 2 cans (5 ounces *each*) **SWANSON** Premium Chunk White *or* Chunk Chicken for cubed cooked chicken.

Turkey Scaloppine

     1 tablespoon vegetable oil
     1 pound turkey breast cutlets or slices
     1 medium onion, chopped (about ½ cup)
     ½ teaspoon dried rosemary leaves, crushed
     ¼ teaspoon garlic powder or 2 cloves garlic, minced
     ⅛ teaspoon pepper
     1 jar (12 ounces) PEPPERIDGE FARM Seasoned Turkey Gravy
     4 cups hot cooked egg noodles (about 4 cups dry)

• In medium skillet over medium-high heat, heat oil. Add turkey in 2 batches and cook
3 minutes or until lightly browned. Set turkey aside.

• Reduce heat to medium. Add onion, rosemary, garlic powder and pepper and cook until tender.

• Add gravy. Heat to a boil. Return turkey to pan. Reduce heat to low. Cover and cook 5 minutes
or until turkey is no longer pink. Serve with noodles. If desired, garnish with *fresh rosemary*.

Makes 4 servings • Prep Time: 10 minutes • Cook Time: 20 minutes

Beefy Vegetable Turnovers

     1 package PEPPERIDGE FARM frozen Puff Pastry Sheets (2 sheets)
     1 pound ground beef
     1 medium onion, chopped (about ½ cup)
     1 jar (12 ounces) PEPPERIDGE FARM Hearty Beef Gravy
     1 teaspoon Worcestershire sauce
     ½ teaspoon dried thyme leaves, crushed
     ⅛ teaspoon garlic powder
  1½ cups frozen mixed vegetables, thawed

• Thaw pastry sheets at room temperature 30 minutes. Preheat oven to 400°F.

• In medium skillet over medium-high heat, cook beef and onion until beef is browned.
Pour off fat. Add gravy, Worcestershire, thyme, garlic powder and vegetables.

• Unfold pastry on floured surface. Roll each sheet into 12-inch square and cut into 4 (6-inch)
squares. Place about ½ cup beef mixture in center of each square. Brush edges of squares with
water. Fold squares to form triangles. Seal edges with fork. Place on 2 baking sheets. Bake
25 minutes or until golden.

Makes 8 servings • Thaw Time: 30 minutes
Prep Time: 35 minutes • Cook Time: 25 minutes

Chicken Pot Pie

  1 package **PEPPERIDGE FARM** *frozen Puff Pastry Shells*
  1 tablespoon margarine or butter
  1 medium onion, chopped (about ½ cup)
  1 rib celery, chopped (about ½ cup)
  1 teaspoon poultry seasoning
 ⅛ teaspoon garlic powder or 1 clove garlic, minced
  2 jars (12 ounces each) **PEPPERIDGE FARM** Golden Chicken Gravy
  1 package (16 ounces) frozen vegetable combination
     (broccoli, cauliflower, carrots), thawed
  3 cups cubed cooked chicken

• Thaw pastry shells at room temperature 30 minutes. Preheat oven to 400°F.

• In medium skillet over medium heat, heat margarine. Add onion, celery, poultry seasoning and garlic powder and cook until tender.

• In 3-quart shallow baking dish mix gravy, onion mixture, vegetables and chicken.

• Cut each pastry shell into 6 wedges. Place pastry wedges around edge of casserole. Bake 30 minutes or until pastry is golden. If desired, garnish with *celery leaves*.

Makes 6 servings • Thaw Time: 30 minutes
Prep Time: 15 minutes • Cook Time: 30 minutes

Turkey-Stuffing Bundles

1 package PEPPERIDGE FARM frozen Puff Pastry Sheets (2 sheets)
2 cups cubed cooked turkey or chicken
½ cup cooked vegetable (peas, corn, green beans or carrots)
1 jar (12 ounces) PEPPERIDGE FARM Seasoned Turkey Gravy
2 cups prepared PEPPERIDGE FARM Stuffing, any variety
½ cup cranberry sauce

• Thaw pastry sheets at room temperature 30 minutes. Preheat oven to 400°F. Mix turkey, vegetable and ½ cup gravy and set aside.

• Unfold pastry on lightly floured surface. Roll each sheet into 14-inch square and cut into 4 (7-inch) squares *(fig. A)*. Place ¼ *cup* stuffing in center of each square. Top with about ⅓ *cup* turkey mixture and *1 tablespoon* cranberry sauce. Brush edges of squares with water. Fold corners to center on top of filling *(fig. B)* and pinch edges to seal *(fig. C)*. If desired, flute edges. Place on baking sheets.

• Bake 25 minutes or until golden.

• Heat remaining gravy and serve with bundles. If desired, garnish with *orange, fresh cranberries* and *fresh savory.*

Makes 8 servings • Thaw Time: 30 minutes
Prep Time: 30 minutes • Cook Time: 25 minutes

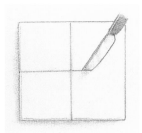

A. Cut each sheet into 4 squares.

B. Fold corners to center on top of filling.

C. Pinch edges to seal.

Parslied Chicken en Croûte

    2 *tablespoons margarine or butter*
    4 *skinless, boneless chicken breast halves (about 1 pound)*
  ½ *package PEPPERIDGE FARM frozen Puff Pastry Sheets (1 sheet)*
    1 *egg, beaten*
    1 *tablespoon water*
    1 *container (4 ounces) herbed cream cheese spread*
  ¼ *cup chopped fresh parsley*

• In medium skillet over medium-high heat, heat margarine. Season chicken with salt and pepper, if desired. Add chicken and cook until browned. Remove chicken from skillet. Cover and refrigerate 15 minutes or up to 24 hours.

• Thaw pastry sheets at room temperature 30 minutes. Mix egg and water and set aside. Preheat oven to 400°F.

• Unfold pastry on lightly floured surface. Roll into 14-inch square and cut into 4 (7-inch) squares. Spread about *2 tablespoons* of the cream cheese in center of each square. Sprinkle with *1 tablespoon* parsley and top with cooled chicken *(fig. A)*. Brush edges of squares with egg mixture. Fold each corner to center on top of chicken *(fig. B)* and seal edges *(fig. C)*. Place seam-side down on baking sheet. Brush with egg mixture.

• Bake 25 minutes or until golden. If desired, garnish with *fresh chives* and additional *fresh parsley.*

Makes 4 servings • Thaw Time: 30 minutes
Prep Time: 20 minutes • Cook Time: 25 minutes

A. Top cheese and parsley with cooled chicken.

B. Fold each corner to center on top of chicken.

C. Pinch together pastry to seal edges.

Crunchy Chicken with Ham Sauce

    1 can (10 ¾ ounces) CAMPBELL'S condensed Cream of Chicken Soup
    ¾ cup milk
    6 skinless, boneless chicken breast halves (about 1½ pounds)
    3 tablespoons all-purpose flour
    2 cups PEPPERIDGE FARM Herb Seasoned Stuffing, crushed
    2 tablespoons margarine or butter, melted
    ½ cup shredded Swiss cheese (2 ounces)
    ⅓ cup chopped cooked ham
    6 cups hot cooked egg noodles (about 6 cups dry), optional

• Mix ⅓ cup soup and ¼ cup milk in shallow dish. Lightly coat chicken with flour. Dip into soup mixture. Coat with stuffing crumbs.

• Place chicken on baking sheet. Drizzle with margarine. Bake at 400°F. for 20 minutes or until chicken is no longer pink.

• In small saucepan mix remaining soup, remaining milk, cheese and ham. Over medium heat, heat until cheese is melted, stirring occasionally. Serve with chicken. If desired, garnish with *tomato* and serve with noodles.

Makes 6 servings • Prep Time: 20 minutes
Cook Time: 20 minutes

Sesame Beef and Peppers

 1 pound boneless beef sirloin or top round steak, ¾ inch thick
 2 tablespoons vegetable oil
 2 small green, sweet red and/or yellow peppers, cut into 2-inch-long strips
   (about 2 cups)
 1 large onion, sliced (about 1⅓ cups)
 ¼ teaspoon garlic powder or 2 cloves garlic, minced (optional)
 1 jar (12 ounces) **PEPPERIDGE FARM** Roasted Onion and Garlic
   or Hearty Beef Gravy
 1 tablespoon soy sauce
 1 tablespoon sesame oil (optional)
 4 cups hot cooked rice

• Slice beef into very thin strips.

• In medium skillet over medium-high heat, heat *half* the vegetable oil. Add beef in 2 batches and stir-fry until browned. Set beef aside.

• Reduce heat to medium. Add remaining vegetable oil. Add peppers, onion and garlic powder and stir-fry until tender-crisp.

• Add gravy, soy sauce and sesame oil. Heat to a boil. Return beef to pan and heat through. Serve over rice. If desired, garnish with *tomatoes* and *green onion*.

Makes 4 servings • Prep Time: 15 minutes
Cook Time: 25 minutes

Easy Beef Stroganoff

     1 package PEPPERIDGE FARM frozen Puff Pastry Shells
     1 pound boneless beef sirloin or top round steak, ¾ inch thick
     2 tablespoons vegetable oil
  1½ cups sliced fresh mushrooms (about 4 ounces)
     1 medium onion, chopped (about ½ cup)
   ½ teaspoon dried thyme leaves, crushed
   ⅛ teaspoon garlic powder or 1 clove garlic, minced
     1 jar (12 ounces) PEPPERIDGE FARM Hearty Beef Gravy
   ½ cup sour cream

• Bake pastry shells according to package directions.

• Slice beef into very thin strips.

• In medium skillet over medium-high heat, heat *half* the oil. Add beef in 2 batches and cook until browned, stirring often. Set beef aside.

• Reduce heat to medium. Add remaining oil. Add mushrooms, onion, thyme and garlic powder and cook until tender.

• Add gravy. Heat to a boil. Reduce heat to low. Stir in sour cream. Return beef to pan and heat through. Serve in pastry shells. If desired, garnish with *assorted sweet peppers* and *fresh thyme.*

Makes 6 servings • Bake Time: 30 minutes
Prep Time: 15 minutes • Cook Time: 25 minutes

Make-Ahead Pizza Meat Loaves

        1 jar (28 ounces) PREGO Traditional Spaghetti Sauce
    1½ pounds ground beef
    1½ cups PEPPERIDGE FARM Herb Seasoned Stuffing
        2 eggs, beaten
        1 medium onion, chopped (about ½ cup)
      ¼ cup chopped green pepper
        1 teaspoon dried oregano leaves, crushed
        4 ounces mozzarella cheese, cut into 6 pieces

• Mix ¾ cup spaghetti sauce, beef, stuffing, eggs, onion, pepper and oregano *thoroughly*. Shape *firmly* into 6 loaves, placing a cheese piece in center of each. Place loaves in shallow baking pan.

• Bake at 400°F. for 30 minutes or until meat loaves are no longer pink. Cool slightly. Wrap and refrigerate up to 3 days. Cover and refrigerate remaining spaghetti sauce.

• To reheat, in large skillet place meat loaves and remaining spaghetti sauce. Cover. Over medium heat, heat 20 minutes or until hot. If desired, garnish with *tomato* and *fresh oregano*.

Makes 6 servings • Prep Time: 15 minutes
Cook Time: 30 minutes

TIP: Prepare meat mixture as above using ½ cup spaghetti sauce and cutting cheese into 18 pieces. In medium baking pan shape *firmly* into 8- by 4-inch loaf. Press cheese pieces into loaf, covering with meat mixture. Bake at 350°F. for 1 hour or until meat loaf is no longer pink (160°F. internal temperature). Heat remaining spaghetti sauce and serve with meat loaf.

Caesar Salad *(top, recipe page 74)*
Make-Ahead Pizza Meat Loaves *(bottom)*

Spicy Beef and Broccoli

½ package **PEPPERIDGE FARM** *frozen Puff Pastry Sheets (1 sheet)*
1 pound boneless beef sirloin or top round steak, ¾ inch thick
2 tablespoons cornstarch
1 can (14½ ounces) **SWANSON** *Beef Broth*
1 tablespoon soy sauce
½ teaspoon crushed red pepper
2 tablespoons vegetable oil
4 cups fresh broccoli flowerets
2 green onions, sliced (about ¼ cup)

• Thaw pastry sheet at room temperature 30 minutes. Preheat oven to 400°F.

• Unfold pastry on lightly floured surface. Cut into 4 squares. Cut 3-inch slits from corners to centers of squares *(fig. A)*. Fold every other point to center to form a pinwheel *(fig. B)*. Press firmly to seal *(fig. C)*. Place on baking sheet. Bake 15 minutes or until golden.

• Slice beef into very thin strips. In cup mix cornstarch, broth, soy sauce and pepper until smooth and set aside.

• In medium skillet over medium-high heat, heat *half* the oil. Add beef in 2 batches and stir-fry until browned. Set beef aside.

• Reduce heat to medium. Add remaining oil. Add broccoli and onions and stir-fry until tender-crisp.

• Stir cornstarch mixture and add. Cook until mixture boils and thickens, stirring constantly. Return beef to pan and heat through. Serve over baked pastry pinwheels. If desired, garnish with *sweet red pepper* and *fresh thyme*.

Makes 4 servings • Thaw Time: 30 minutes • Prep Time: 15 minutes • Cook Time: 25 minutes

A. Cut 3-inch slits from corners to center of squares.

B. Fold every other point to center to form a pinwheel.

C. Press firmly on center to seal.

Grilled Orange Beef

  1 jar (12 ounces) PEPPERIDGE FARM *Hearty Beef Gravy*
  1 tablespoon orange peel cut in 1-inch-long very thin strips
  2 tablespoons orange juice
  ¼ teaspoon garlic powder or 2 cloves garlic, minced
  1½ pounds boneless beef top round steak, 1½ inches thick

• Mix gravy, orange strips, orange juice and garlic powder and set aside.

• Place steak on lightly oiled grill rack directly over medium-hot coals. Grill to desired doneness (allow 25 minutes for medium), turning once and brushing often with gravy mixture. Thinly slice steak.

• Heat remaining gravy mixture to a boil and serve with steak. If desired, garnish with *orange peel, orange slices* and *fresh dill.*

  Makes 6 servings • Prep Time: 10 minutes • Cook Time: 25 minutes

Pastry Tostadas Olé

  1 package PEPPERIDGE FARM *frozen Puff Pastry Shells*
  1 pound ground beef
  ¾ cup water
  1 package (about 1¼ ounces) taco seasoning mix
  1 cup shredded Cheddar or Monterey Jack cheese (4 ounces)
  1 medium tomato, chopped (about 1 cup)
  ¼ cup sliced VLASIC or EARLY CALIFORNIA *pitted Ripe Olives*
  2 green onions, sliced (about ¼ cup)

• Thaw pastry shells at room temperature 30 minutes. Preheat oven to 400°F.

• Roll pastry shells into 7-inch circles on lightly floured surface. Place on 2 baking sheets and prick *thoroughly* with fork. Bake 15 minutes or until golden.

• Meanwhile, in medium skillet over medium-high heat, cook beef until browned, stirring to separate meat. Pour off fat. Add water and taco seasoning. Heat to a boil. Reduce heat to low and cook 5 minutes.

• Divide beef mixture among baked pastry circles. Top with cheese, tomato, olives and onions. If desired, garnish with *sour cream, lime, hot peppers* and *fresh cilantro.*

  Makes 6 servings • Thaw Time: 30 minutes
  Prep Time: 15 minutes • Cook Time: 15 minutes

Sweet-and-Sour Stuffed Pork Chops

6 boneless pork chops, 1¼ inches thick (about 2 pounds)
1 can (8 ounces) crushed pineapple, undrained
½ cup water
1 rib celery, chopped (about ½ cup)
¼ cup margarine or butter
2 tablespoons packed brown sugar
2 tablespoons soy sauce
1 tablespoon vinegar
¼ teaspoon garlic powder
1 package (8 ounces) PEPPERIDGE FARM Corn Bread Stuffing

• Cut pocket in each chop and set aside.

• In medium saucepan mix *undrained* pineapple, water, celery, margarine, sugar, soy sauce, vinegar and garlic powder. Over medium heat, heat to a boil. Remove from heat. Add stuffing and mix lightly.

• Spoon stuffing mixture into pork chop pockets. Place chops stuffing-side up in 2-quart shallow baking dish. Cover.

• Bake at 350°F. for 20 minutes. Uncover and bake 25 minutes more or until chops are no longer pink. If desired, garnish with *assorted sweet peppers* and *fresh sage*.

Makes 6 servings • Prep Time: 15 minutes
Cook Time: 45 minutes

TIP: Substitute 6 pork chops, ¾ inch thick (about 2 pounds) for boneless pork chops. Prepare stuffing as above but spoon into greased 2-quart shallow baking dish and top with chops. Bake at 400°F. for 40 minutes or until chops are no longer pink.

Ham-and-Cheese Florentine

½ package PEPPERIDGE FARM frozen Puff Pastry Sheets (1 sheet)
1 egg, beaten
1 tablespoon water
2 green onions, chopped (about ¼ cup)
2 tablespoons chopped pimiento (optional)
½ teaspoon dried oregano leaves, crushed
½ pound sliced cooked ham
½ pound sliced cooked turkey
1 cup fresh spinach leaves
4 ounces sliced Swiss cheese

• Thaw pastry sheet at room temperature 30 minutes. Preheat oven to 400°F. Mix egg and water and set aside. Mix onions, pimiento and oregano and set aside.

• Unfold pastry on lightly floured surface. Roll into 16- by 12-inch rectangle. With short side facing you, layer ham, turkey, spinach and cheese on bottom half of pastry to within 1 inch of edges. Sprinkle with onion mixture *(fig. A)*. Starting at short side, roll up like a jelly roll *(fig. B)*. Place seam-side down on baking sheet. Tuck ends under to seal *(fig. C)*. Brush with egg mixture.

• Bake 25 minutes or until golden. Slice and serve warm. If desired, garnish with *fresh oregano*.

Makes 6 servings • Thaw Time: 30 minutes
Prep Time: 20 minutes • Cook Time: 25 minutes

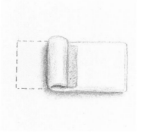

A. Sprinkle with onion mixture.

B. Starting at short side, roll up like a jelly roll.

C. Tuck ends under to seal.

Seafood au Gratin

      1 package PEPPERIDGE FARM frozen Puff Pastry Shells
    ¼ cup margarine or butter
    ½ pound medium shrimp, shelled and deveined
    ½ pound scallops, cut into halves
      2 cups sliced fresh mushrooms (about 6 ounces)
    ¼ teaspoon garlic powder or 2 cloves garlic, minced
      2 tablespoons all-purpose flour
  1½ cups milk
      1 cup shredded Swiss cheese (4 ounces)
      2 tablespoons chopped fresh parsley

• Bake pastry shells according to package directions.

• In skillet over medium-high heat, heat *half* the margarine. Add shrimp and scallops in 2 batches and cook until seafood is opaque. Set aside.

• Reduce heat to medium. Add mushrooms and garlic and cook until tender. Set aside. Add remaining margarine. Stir in flour until smooth. Add milk and cook until mixture boils and thickens, stirring constantly. Cook 2 minutes.

• Reduce heat to low. Add cheese and parsley and stir until cheese is melted. Return seafood and mushrooms to pan and heat through. Serve in pastry shells. If desired, garnish with additional *fresh parsley*.

Makes 6 servings • Bake Time: 30 minutes • Prep Time: 20 minutes • Cook Time: 20 minutes

Herbed Crab Cakes

  1½ cups PEPPERIDGE FARM Herb Seasoned Stuffing
      2 eggs, beaten
    ⅓ cup mayonnaise
      2 teaspoons Dijon-style mustard
      1 teaspoon Worcestershire sauce
      1 tablespoon chopped fresh parsley
      1 can (16 ounces) refrigerated pasteurized crab meat
      2 tablespoons margarine or butter

• Crush ½ cup stuffing; set aside. Mix *lightly* remaining stuffing and next 6 ingredients. Shape into 6 (3-inch) patties. Coat with stuffing crumbs.

• In medium skillet over medium heat, heat margarine. Cook patties in 2 batches 5 minutes or until hot. (Use additional margarine if necessary.) Serve with *lemon wedges*. If desired, garnish with *fresh dill*.

Makes 6 servings • Prep Time: 5 minutes • Cook Time: 10 minutes

Seafood au Gratin *(top)*
Herbed Crab Cakes *(bottom)*

Vegetable-Cheese Strudel

½ package PEPPERIDGE FARM frozen Puff Pastry Sheets (1 sheet)
1 egg, beaten
1 tablespoon water
2 tablespoons vegetable oil
2 small green or sweet red peppers, cut into 2-inch-long strips
1 cup sliced fresh mushrooms (about 3 ounces)
1 cup cubed eggplant
1 small onion, sliced (about ½ cup)
1 teaspoon dried basil leaves, crushed
¼ teaspoon garlic powder or 2 cloves garlic, minced
4 ounces mozzarella cheese, cut into 8 slices

• Thaw pastry sheet at room temperature 30 minutes. Preheat oven to 400°F. Mix egg and water and set aside.

• In medium skillet over medium-high heat, heat oil. Add next 6 ingredients and cook until tender. Cool to room temperature.

• Unfold pastry on lightly floured surface. Roll into 16- by 12-inch rectangle. With short side facing you, spoon vegetable mixture on bottom half of pastry to within 1 inch of edges *(fig. A)*. Top with cheese. Starting at short side, roll up like a jelly roll *(fig. B)*. Place seam-side down on baking sheet *(fig. C)*. Tuck ends under to seal. Brush with egg mixture. If desired, for decorative top, see tip below.

• Bake 25 minutes or until golden. Slice and serve warm. If desired, garnish with *tomato* and *watercress*.

Makes 6 servings • Thaw Time: 30 minutes • Prep Time: 35 minutes • Cook Time: 35 minutes

TIP: To make decorative cut-outs, use remaining pastry sheet. Thaw and cut into desired shapes. Press onto top of strudel. Brush tops with egg mixture. Bake as directed above.

A. Spoon vegetable mixture on bottom half of pastry.

B. Starting at short side, roll up like a jelly roll.

C. Place seam-side down on baking sheet.

Easy Eggs Benedict

    1 package PEPPERIDGE FARM *frozen Puff Pastry Shells*
    1 to 1½ cups Hollandaise sauce (homemade or prepared packaged mix)
    6 slices Canadian-style bacon (about 6 ounces)
    1 tablespoon margarine or butter
    6 eggs, beaten
    1 green onion, chopped (about 2 tablespoons)

• Bake pastry shells according to package directions, but *do not remove centers.* Prepare Hollandaise sauce and keep warm.

• In skillet over medium heat, cook bacon until browned. Remove; keep warm.

• In same skillet over medium heat, heat margarine. Add eggs and onion and cook until eggs are just set, stirring often.

• Cut baked pastry shells crosswise into halves. Place bacon on pastry shell bottoms. Top with egg mixture and remaining pastry shell halves. Spoon Hollandaise sauce over pastry shells. If desired, garnish with *green onion.*

Makes 6 servings • Bake Time: 25 minutes
Prep Time: 10 minutes • Cook Time: 15 minutes

Cheddar-Ham Rarebit

    1 package PEPPERIDGE FARM *frozen Puff Pastry Shells*
    ¾ cup cubed cooked ham
    1 can (10 ¾ ounces) CAMPBELL'S *condensed Cheddar Cheese Soup*
    ⅓ cup milk
    2 teaspoons Worcestershire sauce
    ½ teaspoon dry mustard
    2 small tomatoes, cut into 6 slices

• Bake pastry shells according to package directions. Immediately fill each shell with *2 tablespoons* ham.

• In saucepan mix next 4 ingredients. Over medium heat, heat through.

• Top shells with tomato slices. Pour soup mixture over tomatoes and sprinkle with *paprika.* If desired, garnish with *fresh chives.*

Makes 6 servings • Bake Time: 30 minutes
Prep Time: 10 minutes • Cook Time: 5 minutes

Easy Eggs Benedict *(top)*
Cheddar-Ham Rarebit *(bottom)*

Spectacular Sides

Savory side dishes mean home-style harmony on your table. Whether it's *Spinach-Mushroom Salad, Squash Casserole* or delectably different *Vegetable-Dill Stuffing*, Pepperidge Farm blends the simplicity of ingredients with the homemade goodness of simpler times.

Spinach-Mushroom Salad (top, page 71) and *Potato Strudel* (bottom, page 70).

Potato Strudel

Quick Mashed Potatoes (recipe follows)
¼ teaspoon garlic powder
1 green onion, chopped (about 2 tablespoons)
4 slices bacon, cooked and crumbled (optional)
½ package PEPPERIDGE FARM frozen Puff Pastry Sheets (1 sheet)
1 egg, beaten
1 tablespoon water
1 jar (12 ounces) PEPPERIDGE FARM Gravy, any flavor

• Mix potatoes, garlic powder, onion and bacon and cool to room temperature. Thaw pastry sheet at room temperature 30 minutes. Preheat oven to 400°F. Mix egg and water and set aside.

• Unfold pastry on lightly floured surface. Roll into 16- by 12-inch rectangle. With short side facing you, spoon potato mixture on bottom half of pastry to within 1 inch of edges. Starting at short side, roll up like a jelly roll. Place seam-side down on baking sheet. Tuck ends under to seal. Brush with egg mixture.

• Bake 25 minutes or until golden. Heat gravy and serve with strudel. If desired, garnish with *green onions* and *grapes*.

Makes 8 servings • Thaw Time: 30 minutes
Prep Time: 25 minutes • Cook Time: 25 minutes

Quick Mashed Potatoes: In medium saucepan heat *3 cups water* and *3 tablespoons margarine or butter* to a boil. Stir in *¾ cup milk* and *½ teaspoon salt* (optional). Stir in *4 cups instant mashed potato flakes or buds* until water is absorbed.

Spinach-Mushroom Salad

1 package (10 ounces) fresh spinach leaves, washed and torn into bite-size pieces
2 cups PEPPERIDGE FARM Home Style Sourdough Cheese Croutons
2 cups sliced fresh mushrooms (about 6 ounces)
6 slices bacon, cooked and crumbled
1 medium red onion, thinly sliced (about 3/4 cup)
2 hard-cooked eggs, sliced
3/4 cup vegetable oil
3 tablespoons vinegar
2 teaspoons sugar
1/2 teaspoon dry mustard

• In large bowl toss spinach, croutons, mushrooms, bacon, onion and eggs.

• In small saucepan mix oil, vinegar, sugar and mustard. Over medium-high heat, heat through. Add to spinach mixture and toss until evenly coated.

Makes about 8 cups or 8 servings • Prep Time: 30 minutes

TIP: Dressing can be heated in the microwave. In 1-cup microwave-safe measuring cup, mix oil, vinegar, sugar and mustard. Microwave on HIGH 1 minute or until hot.

Say Stuffing— *Any Day of the Week!*

Country Garden Stuffing

1 bag (16 ounces) frozen vegetable combination (broccoli, cauliflower, carrots)
¾ cup water
4 cups PEPPERIDGE FARM Cubed Country Style Stuffing
1 jar (12 ounces) PEPPERIDGE FARM Golden Chicken Gravy

• In large saucepan place vegetables and water. Over high heat, heat to a boil. Remove from heat.

• Add stuffing and gravy. Mix lightly. Spoon into greased 2-quart casserole. Bake at 350°F. for 25 minutes or until hot. Serve with poultry or pork.

Makes about 6 cups or 6 servings
Prep Time: 10 minutes
Cook Time: 25 minutes

Sausage Corn Bread Stuffing

¼ pound bulk pork sausage
1¼ cups water
1 bag (8 ounces) PEPPERIDGE FARM Corn Bread Stuffing
½ cup shredded Cheddar cheese (2 ounces)
½ cup cooked whole kernel corn
1 tablespoon chopped fresh parsley or 1 teaspoon dried parsley flakes

• In large saucepan over medium-high heat, cook sausage until browned, stirring to separate meat. Spoon off fat.

• Add water. Heat to a boil. Remove from heat. Add stuffing, cheese, corn and parsley. Mix lightly. Spoon into greased 1½-quart casserole. Bake at 350°F. for 25 minutes or until hot. Serve with pork, ham or poultry.

Makes about 6 cups or 6 servings
Prep Time: 15 minutes
Cook Time: 25 minutes

*Y*ou don't have to wait until Thanksgiving to serve stuffing. Pepperidge Farm *country style*, *herb seasoned* and *corn bread* stuffing can all be prepared on top of the stove, in only minutes! Add a few additional ingredients to create tempting stuffings like the ones featured here.

Apple-Raisin Stuffing

- ¼ cup margarine or butter
- 1 rib celery, chopped
- 1 small onion, chopped
- 1 can (10 ½ ounces) CAMPBELL'S condensed Chicken Broth
- 1 bag (7 ounces) PEPPERIDGE FARM Cubed Herb Seasoned Stuffing
- 1 medium apple, cored and chopped (about 1 cup)
- ¼ cup raisins
- ¼ teaspoon ground cinnamon

• In large saucepan over medium heat, heat margarine. Add celery and onion and cook until tender.

• Add broth. Heat to a boil. Remove from heat. Add stuffing, apple, raisins and cinnamon. Mix lightly. Spoon into greased 1½-quart casserole. Bake at 350°F. for 25 minutes or until hot. Serve with poultry, pork or ham.

Makes about 4 cups or 4 servings
Prep Time: 15 minutes
Cook Time: 25 minutes

Vegetable-Dill Stuffing

- ¼ cup margarine or butter
- 2 ribs celery, chopped (about 1 cup)
- 2 tablespoons chopped onion
- 1 can (14½ ounces) SWANSON Vegetable Broth
- 1 bag (8 ounces) PEPPERIDGE FARM Herb Seasoned Stuffing
- ⅓ cup VLASIC Dill Relish

• In large saucepan over medium heat, heat margarine. Add celery and onion and cook until tender.

• Add broth. Heat to a boil. Remove from heat. Add stuffing and relish. Mix lightly. Let stand covered 5 minutes. Serve with fish or poultry.

Makes about 5½ cups or 6 servings
Prep Time: 10 minutes
Cook Time: 15 minutes
Stand Time: 5 minutes

Squash Casserole

   3 cups PEPPERIDGE FARM Corn Bread or Herb Seasoned Stuffing
   ¼ cup margarine or butter, melted
   1 can (10 ¾ ounces) CAMPBELL'S condensed Cream of Chicken Soup
   ½ cup sour cream
   ½ cup shredded Cheddar cheese (2 ounces)
   4 cups shredded zucchini and/or yellow squash (about 4 small)
   ¼ cup shredded carrot

• Mix stuffing and margarine. Reserve ½ cup stuffing mixture. Spread remaining stuffing mixture in greased 2-quart shallow baking dish.

• Mix soup, sour cream, cheese, zucchini and carrot. Spread soup mixture over stuffing mixture. Sprinkle with reserved stuffing mixture.

• Bake at 350°F. for 40 minutes or until hot.

Makes about 6 cups or 8 servings • Prep Time: 20 minutes
Cook Time: 40 minutes

Caesar Salad

   ⅓ cup vegetable oil
   ¼ cup mayonnaise
   1 can (2 ounces) flat anchovies, drained
   2 tablespoons vinegar
   2 tablespoons water
   1 clove garlic, cut in half
   6 cups romaine lettuce torn in bite-size pieces
   2 green onions, sliced (about ¼ cup)
   ¼ cup grated Parmesan cheese
   2 cups PEPPERIDGE FARM Home Style Classic Caesar Croutons

• In blender jar place oil, mayonnaise, anchovies, vinegar, water and garlic. Cover and blend until smooth.

• In large bowl toss romaine, onions, cheese, croutons and dressing mixture until evenly coated.

Makes about 6 cups or 6 servings • Prep Time: 15 minutes

Dazzling Desserts

Your guests are already aglow, so what do you do for an encore?

Let Pepperidge Farm be the icing on the cake with easy, elegant desserts—*Chocolate Sundaes, Apple Strudel, Lemon Tarts, Strawberries Bonaparte, Chocolate Mousse Napoleons* and more. Your final course of action will be a sunny reminder that the sweetest things in life are worth the wait!

Chocolate Bundles (left, page 78) and *Citrus Fruit Tart* (right, page 79).

Chocolate Bundles

½ package PEPPERIDGE FARM frozen Puff Pastry Sheets (1 sheet)
1 package (6 ounces) semisweet chocolate pieces
¼ cup chopped walnuts
Confectioners' sugar

• Thaw pastry sheet at room temperature 30 minutes. Preheat oven to 400°F. Mix chocolate pieces and walnuts and set aside.

• Unfold pastry on lightly floured surface. Roll into 12-inch square. Cut into 9 (4-inch) squares. Place about *2 tablespoons* chocolate mixture in center of each square. Brush edges of squares with water *(fig. A)*. Fold corners to center on top of filling and twist tightly to seal *(fig. B)*. Fan out corners *(fig. C)*. Place 2 inches apart on baking sheet.

• Bake 15 minutes or until golden. Remove from baking sheet and cool on wire rack 10 minutes. Sprinkle with confectioners' sugar. If desired, garnish with *fresh raspberries, chocolate curls* and *fresh mint*.

Makes 9 servings • Thaw Time: 30 minutes
Prep Time: 15 minutes • Cook Time: 15 minutes

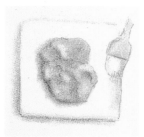

A. Brush edges of squares with water.

B. Fold edges to center on top of filling and twist tightly to seal.

C. Fan out corners.

Citrus Fruit Tart

½ package **PEPPERIDGE FARM** *frozen Puff Pastry Sheets (1 sheet)*
1 package (8 ounces) cream cheese, softened
1 tablespoon sugar
2 tablespoons orange juice
2 teaspoons grated orange peel
1 pint strawberries, cut in half
2 oranges, peeled, cut in half and sliced
2 kiwi fruit, peeled and sliced
½ cup orange marmalade, warmed

• Thaw pastry sheet at room temperature 30 minutes. Preheat oven to 400°F.

• Unfold pastry on lightly floured surface. Roll into 14- by 10-inch rectangle. Brush edges of rectangle with water. Fold over edge ½ inch on all sides and press *firmly* to form rim. Inside rim, prick pastry *thoroughly* with fork. Bake 15 minutes or until golden. (After 10 minutes baking time break any large air bubbles with fork.) Remove from baking sheet. Cool on wire rack.

• Mix cream cheese, sugar, orange juice and orange peel. Spread on pastry. Arrange strawberries, oranges and kiwi fruit on cheese mixture. Spoon marmalade over fruit. Cover and refrigerate at least 4 hours until serving time. Cut into rectangles. If desired, garnish with *fresh strawberries* and *orange peel.*

Makes 12 servings • Thaw Time: 30 minutes
Prep Time: 30 minutes • Cook Time: 15 minutes

TIP: For round tart, thaw and unfold pastry as above. Roll into 13-inch square and trim to make 13-inch circle. Place on 12-inch pizza pan or baking sheet. Brush edge of circle with water. Fold over edge ½ inch and press firmly to make rim. Bake as directed.

Chocolate Sundaes

    1 *package PEPPERIDGE FARM frozen Puff Pastry Shells*
    1 *package (6 ounces) semisweet chocolate pieces*
    6 *tablespoons margarine or butter*
    1 *pint vanilla ice cream (2 cups)*
    ¼ *cup finely chopped walnuts*

• Bake and cool pastry shells according to package directions.

• In medium saucepan place chocolate and margarine. Over low heat, heat until chocolate softens. Stir until smooth.

• Place a scoop of ice cream in each pastry shell and place on 6 dessert plates. Spoon warm chocolate mixture over ice cream. Sprinkle with nuts. (Chocolate mixture will harden making a "chocolate shell.") If desired, garnish with *fresh mint.*

Makes 6 servings • Bake Time: 30 minutes • Prep Time: 10 minutes

Peach Sorbet Melba

    1 *package PEPPERIDGE FARM frozen Puff Pastry Shells*
    ⅓ *cup sugar*
    2 *tablespoons cornstarch*
    ½ *cup water*
    1 *package (10 ounces) frozen raspberries*
    1 *pint peach, raspberry or strawberry sorbet or sherbet (2 cups)*
    4 *medium peaches, peeled, pitted and sliced (about 2 cups)*
    1 *tablespoon sugar*
    1 *teaspoon lemon juice*

• Bake and cool pastry shells according to package directions.

• In small saucepan mix ⅓ *cup* sugar, cornstarch, water and raspberries. Over medium heat cook until mixture boils and thickens, stirring constantly. Remove from heat and press raspberry mixture through sieve. Cool to room temperature.

• In bowl, mix peaches, *1 tablespoon* sugar and lemon juice. Set aside.

• On each of 6 dessert plates, pour about *1 tablespoon* raspberry mixture and tilt plate to coat. Place a scoop of sorbet in each shell and place on prepared plates. Divide peach slices among plates and spoon remaining raspberry sauce over sorbet. If desired, garnish with *fresh raspberries.*

Makes 6 servings • Bake Time: 30 minutes • Prep Time: 15 minutes

Chocolate Sundaes *(top)*
Peach Sorbet Melba *(bottom)*

Apple Strudel

½ *package* **PEPPERIDGE FARM** *frozen Puff Pastry Sheets (1 sheet)*
1 *egg, beaten*
1 *tablespoon water*
2 *tablespoons sugar*
1 *tablespoon all-purpose flour*
¼ *teaspoon ground cinnamon*
2 *large Granny Smith apples, peeled, cored and thinly sliced (about 3 cups)*
2 *tablespoons raisins*

• Thaw pastry sheet at room temperature 30 minutes. Preheat oven to 375°F. Mix egg and water and set aside. Mix sugar, flour and cinnamon. Add apples and raisins and toss to coat and set aside.

•Unfold pastry on lightly floured surface. Roll into 16- by 12-inch rectangle. With short side facing you, spoon apple mixture on bottom half of pastry to within 1 inch of edges. Starting at short side, roll up like a jelly roll. Place seam-side down on baking sheet. Tuck ends under to seal. Brush with egg mixture. Cut several 2-inch-long slits 2 inches apart on top.

• Bake 35 minutes or until golden. Cool on baking sheet on wire rack about 30 minutes before serving. Slice and serve warm. If desired, sprinkle with *confectioners' sugar* and garnish with *fresh mint.*

Makes 6 servings • Thaw Time: 30 minutes
Prep Time: 30 minutes • Cook Time: 35 minutes

Apple Strudel

Strawberries Bonaparte

½ package PEPPERIDGE FARM frozen Puff Pastry Sheets (1 sheet)
1 package (about 3½ ounces) vanilla instant pudding mix
1 cup milk
1 cup heavy cream, whipped or 2 cups thawed frozen non-dairy
    or dairy whipped topping
½ cup confectioners' sugar
2 teaspoons milk
1½ cups sliced fresh strawberries

• Thaw pastry sheet at room temperature 30 minutes. Preheat oven to 400°F.

• Unfold pastry on lightly floured surface. Cut into 3 strips along fold marks. Place on baking sheet. Bake 15 minutes or until golden. Remove from baking sheet and cool on wire rack.

• Prepare pudding mix according to package directions with *1 cup* milk. Fold in whipped cream. Cover and refrigerate. In small bowl mix confectioners' sugar and *2 teaspoons* milk and set aside.

• Split pastries into 2 layers, making 6 layers in all. On 2 top layers, spread icing.

• Spread 1 pastry layer with ¾ *cup* pudding mixture. Top with about ⅓ *cup* strawberries. Repeat layers. Top with iced pastry layer. Repeat to make second dessert. Serve immediately or cover and refrigerate up to 4 hours. If desired, garnish with *edible flowers*.

TIP: For easier slicing, refrigerate 1 hour and use a wet serrated knife.

Makes 12 servings • Thaw Time: 30 minutes
Prep Time: 25 minutes • Cook Time: 15 minutes

Berry Bordeaux Desserts

   1 cup heavy cream
   ¼ cup sugar
   1 teaspoon vanilla
  24 **PEPPERIDGE FARM** Distinctive Bordeaux Cookies
   3 cups mixed berries (sliced strawberries, raspberries, blackberries
       and/or blueberries)

• In small bowl place cream, *2 tablespoons* sugar and vanilla. Beat with electric mixer at high speed until stiff peaks form. Spoon or pipe whipped cream mixture on 12 cookies. Top with remaining cookies. Cover and refrigerate until cookies soften, about 3 hours.

• Mix berries with remaining sugar. On dessert plates place cream-filled cookies and serve with berry mixture. If desired, garnish with *fresh mint.*

Makes 12 servings • Prep Time: 20 minutes • Chill Time: 3 hours

Southern Pecan Crisps

  ½ package **PEPPERIDGE FARM** *frozen Puff Pastry Sheets (1 sheet)*
  ½ cup packed brown sugar
   2 tablespoons margarine or butter, melted
  ⅓ cup chopped pecans
     Confectioners' sugar

• Thaw pastry sheet at room temperature 30 minutes. Preheat oven to 400°F. Mix sugar, margarine and pecans and set aside.

• Unfold pastry on lightly floured surface. Roll into 15- by 12-inch rectangle. Cut into 20 (3-inch) squares. Press squares into bottoms of 3-inch muffin-pan cups. Place *1 heaping teaspoon* pecan mixture in center of each.

• Bake 12 minutes or until golden. Remove and cool on wire rack. Sprinkle with confectioners' sugar. If desired, garnish with *edible flowers* and *lemon peel.*

Makes 20 servings • Thaw Time: 30 minutes
Prep Time: 25 minutes • Cook Time: 12 minutes

Berry Bordeaux Desserts *(top)*
Southern Pecan Crisps *(bottom)*

Chocolate Mousse Napoleons

½ package **PEPPERIDGE FARM** *frozen Puff Pastry Sheets (1 sheet)*
1 cup heavy cream
¼ teaspoon ground cinnamon
1 package (6 ounces) semisweet chocolate pieces, melted and cooled
1 square (1 ounce) semisweet chocolate, melted (optional)
Confectioners' sugar

• Thaw pastry sheet at room temperature 30 minutes. Preheat oven to 400°F.

• Unfold pastry on lightly floured surface. Cut into 3 strips along fold marks *(fig. A)*. Cut each strip into 6 rectangles *(fig. B)*. Place 2 inches apart on baking sheet.

• Bake 15 minutes or until golden. Remove from baking sheet and cool on wire rack.

• In medium bowl place cream and cinnamon. Beat with electric mixer at high speed until stiff peaks form. Fold in melted chocolate pieces. Split pastries into 2 layers. Spread 18 halves with chocolate cream. Top with remaining halves. Cover and refrigerate up to 4 hours.

• Drizzle with melted chocolate and sprinkle with confectioners' sugar.

Makes 18 servings • Thaw Time: 30 minutes
Prep Time: 25 minutes • Cook Time: 15 minutes

A. Cut into 3 strips along fold marks.

B. Cut each strip into 6 rectangles.

Lemon Tarts

1 package PEPPERIDGE FARM frozen Puff Pastry Shells
1 package (about 3 ounces) lemon pudding mix
1 teaspoon grated lemon peel
1 cup sweetened whipped cream or thawed frozen non-dairy whipped topping

• Bake and cool pastry shells according to package directions.

• Prepare pudding mix according to package directions for pie filling. Stir in lemon peel and cool to room temperature.

• Spoon about ⅓ cup pudding into each pastry shell. Top each filled pastry shell with whipped cream. Serve immediately or cover and refrigerate until serving time. If desired, garnish with *lemon peel* and *edible flowers*.

Makes 6 servings • Bake Time: 30 minutes • Prep Time: 20 minutes

Peach Streusel Tart

½ package PEPPERIDGE FARM frozen Puff Pastry Sheets (1 sheet)
1 egg, beaten
1 tablespoon water
9 PEPPERIDGE FARM Distinctive Bordeaux Cookies, crushed
2 tablespoons sugar
1 teaspoon ground cinnamon
2 tablespoons margarine or butter, melted
8 medium peaches, peeled, pitted and sliced (about 4 cups)

• Thaw pastry sheet at room temperature 30 minutes. Preheat oven to 375°F. Mix egg and water and set aside. Mix cookie crumbs, sugar, cinnamon and margarine and set aside.

• Unfold pastry on lightly floured surface. Roll into 13-inch square. Trim to make 13-inch circle. Place on 12-inch pizza pan or baking sheet. Fold over edge ½ inch and press firmly to make rim. Brush with egg mixture. Top with peach slices, overlapping slightly. Sprinkle with cookie mixture.

• Bake 35 minutes or until pastry is golden and peaches are tender. Cool in pan on wire rack. Cut into wedges. If desired, garnish with *fresh raspberries* and *fresh mint*.

Makes 8 servings • Thaw Time: 30 minutes
Prep Time: 25 minutes • Cook Time: 35 minutes

Lemon Tarts (*top*)
Peach Streusel Tart (*bottom*)

Chocolate-Cinnamon Bread Pudding

    6 cups cubed PEPPERIDGE FARM Cinnamon Swirl Bread
    1/2 cup semisweet chocolate pieces or raisins
    2 1/2 cups milk
    4 eggs, beaten
    1/2 cup packed brown sugar
    1 teaspoon vanilla
      Sweetened whipped cream (optional)

• In greased 2-quart shallow baking dish place bread cubes. Sprinkle with chocolate pieces. Mix milk, eggs, sugar and vanilla. Pour over bread cubes.

• Bake at 350°F. for 40 minutes or until knife inserted near center comes out clean. Serve warm with *whipped cream*.

Makes 6 servings • Prep Time: 15 minutes • Cook Time: 40 minutes

Coffee Praline Puffs

    1 package PEPPERIDGE FARM frozen Puff Pastry Shells
    2 teaspoons instant coffee powder or granules
    1 teaspoon hot water
    1 tablespoon sugar
    1 cup heavy cream
    2 bars (about 1 1/2 ounces each) chocolate-covered English toffee, crushed (1/2 cup)
    1 bar (1 ounce) milk chocolate, cut into curls

• Bake and cool pastry shells according to package directions.

• Mix coffee and water until dissolved. In medium bowl mix coffee mixture, sugar and cream. Beat with electric mixer at high speed until stiff peaks form. Fold in crushed candy. Divide mixture among pastry shells. Top with chocolate curls. Cover and refrigerate at least 1 hour. If desired, garnish with *fresh fruit* and *fresh mint*.

Makes 6 servings • Bake Time: 30 minutes
Prep Time: 15 minutes • Chill Time: 1 hour

Chocolate-Cinnamon Bread Pudding (*top*)
Coffee Praline Puffs (*bottom*)

Recipe Index

Recipe Index
Continued

Recipes By Product Index